Sourdough Starter

A Beginners Guide to Making Sourdough Bread

Elizabeth May

Table of Contents

Introduction

Congratulations on purchasing *Sourdough Starter,* and thank you for doing so.

The following chapters will discuss the beauty of making your own sourdough bread. There are thousands of great recipes out there that you can choose to use to make bread. But if you want something that has its own unique taste and something that is completely your own and won't match anything else out there, then this is the guidebook for you. We will spend time learning about why sourdough is the best option for any type of bread, we will look at how to make our own sourdough starter, and then we will explore some of the best recipes that you can enjoy when you use this starter!

The first few chapters will be a quick introduction to make sure we are on the same page and ready to take on sourdough bread making. We will talk about the benefits of using sourdough starter, and discuss how to make a really simple starter for your bread. There are many different sourdough starter options, and you will probably find the one that is your favorite. But this will show us just how simple making one of these starters can really be. We will then move on to looking at how to prepare your kitchen and some of the supplies you need to make sure you get the best results each time.

Then it is time for the baking! The rest of this guidebook will spend time looking at the basics of baking sourdough bread, and what steps you need to take to make sure you can create some tasty and delicious bread in no time. We will look at all kinds of bread from your very own artisan varieties to sweet breads, to whole-grain breads and more. When you are done, you will be so happy at the taste, texture, and skill levels that you were able to master, and you will love many of the breads that you can make inside!

Sourdough bread is completely unique, and there isn't anything quite like it out there. Learning how to make this bread, and how to create something that is your own masterpiece can take some time, but with the sourdough bread starter that we have in this guidebook, and some of the tasty recipes that you can choose from, it won't take long to make this a reality. When you are ready to learn more about making your own sourdough bread,this guidebook will get you started!

There are plenty of books on this subject on the market, thanks again for choosing this one! Every effort was made to ensure it is full of as much useful information as possible, please enjoy!

Chapter 1:

Making Your Starter

Sourdough starters have been around for centuries, and they aren't just something that professional bakers can work with. The early Egyptians even used these starters to help them make bread, and many families have held onto their own sourdough starters for generations. This kind of starter is created simply by fermenting a mixture of water and flour. The wild yeast that we find in the flour, combined with some of the good bacteria that will develop during the process of fermentation, will cause CO_2 to release. Wild yeast is more resistant to acidic situations, meaning that it is able to withstand the lactic acid created by bacteria through fermentation to aid in the rising of the dough. The starter's fermentation of sugars within the dough itself is what provides it not only the characteristic holes within it but also the unique taste that we recognize with it. However, because it does involve fermentation to create the reactions, this kind of bread does take longer to proof and rise than most other types of traditional bread. Nevertheless, it is a popular option, and for great reason.

This is a reaction that sometimes will take up two a week, but it is what all good bakers will look for when they want to add a starter to their bread dough. The gas bubbles are the part that will help develop holes inside each loaf of bread. It is possible for anyone who has a want to do this to create and maintain a starter for sourdough. It is not difficult, though it does take a little bit of time.

While many people mistake sourdough bread for nothing special, the truth is, that instead of using yeast to react with gluten, such as with regular loaves of bread, you will be utilizing the starter—a paste that is created combining the yeast with bacteria that will create a different experience entirely. Sourdough bread contains less gluten than traditional loaves and also offers both prebiotic and probiotic properties, aiding in the entire digestion process.

Let's explore how to get this done and some of the steps you can follow to make your own sourdough starter.

Why Use the Starter?

The moment that you create this kind of starter is the moment that you can create breads that are completely your own. They will be unique, and there is no one else who can make them or reproduce them in the exact same manner. And this is because you can make the starter fit your own personal needs. By maintaining this starter, you can make not only really delicious breads, but pretty much any other baked good that you would like. As you will see in this guidebook, there are a lot of great baked goods and breads that you can utilize when using your own starter.

The breads, and all the other baked goods, that you want to make with this starter will have a longer shelf life because the starter will be its own culture of microbes that come from lots of good bacteria. This good bacteria will come in and fight off all the bad bacteria that can cause staleness and mold in the bread.

A good starter is also really versatile. You can easily change up the starter that you have by using different grains and flours. You simply need to save some of the original starter so that it can live on, just in case the later starters fail. If you only bake on occasion, then you can freeze or dry this starter before you use it. The good news here is that freezing the sourdough starter won't be a whole lot different than leaving it in the fridge. The main difference is that when the starter is frozen, you do not need to feed it.

If you do choose to freeze your starter, then you need to begin with one cup of active and recently fed starter. By recently fed we mean that it should have been done within the last six to twelve hours. When you are ready to bake the bread, take the starter out of your freezer and give it time to completely defrost. When it is defrosted, you can start it up on the regular feeding schedule that you used before freezing the mix. Once the starter grows and bubbles, which can take up to a week, then it is time to make your bread.

There are so many benefits to using a sourdough starter. Many people assume that they can only make sourdough bread when they use this starter, but there are so many other great uses for it as well. It can make some of the best breads and desserts out there, allows you to make something that is really unique and adds a nice taste to all that you want to do in the process as well.

Maintaining Your Starter

Now, we've mentioned that starters for sourdough can last for years—or even generations, but how is that possible, you may ask? Won't it go bad? Sourdough starter is fermented, much like alcohol. The fermentation, the interaction between sugar and microorganisms, works to not only give that characteristic flavor but also to ensure that the started does not rot. This is because the starter itself is alive. It is able to be sustained, and as long as you do keep it alive, you prevent it from rotting away. Essentially, the yeast and the bacteria will work together, and so long as you feed them with fresh flour, you can actually keep it alive nearly indefinitely. This is exactly how people manage to pass the same starter through their family lines indefinitely, and the starters can even be split up and maintained separately as well using these processes.

A Simple Recipe

There are a lot of options out there when it is time to make your own sourdough starter. But we will take a moment here to create our own simple recipe. You can work with this one when creating some of the breads and baked goods that we will list out in this guidebook, or you can make one that is completely your own.

For this one, we will make our own starter with just three ingredients. These include bread flour that is unbleached, bottled water or pure filtered water, and whole wheat flour. Some start recipes will ask you to get dry yeast, but sourdough purists like the all-natural wild yeast though it takes a few more days to get it useful for bread. Adding in the active or the instant yeast will speed up the process if you need this done faster.

It is also common for some of the sourdough starter recipes to include salt. This is going to be used for flavor or preservation, but often this is not necessary with sourdough. The fermentation that we go for in this will act as a natural form of preservations, which means that the added salt is not really necessary. If you do go for it for some flavoring, then just add it in with the other ingredients when you go to make the bread, and not into the starter.

When you want to make the starter, actually weigh out the flour instead of using a measuring cup. You want all of the ingredients to be weighed well for this to work, and you will quickly find that one cup of flour is not the same as one cup of water. Having this measured out will ensure the starter works the way that you would like.

The basic recipe that you need here is about four ounces or one cup of whole-grain and whole-wheat flour. Then have four ounces or half a cup of the water. Add in the four ounces or 1 cup of unbleached bread flour, and you are good to go. This will then begin to ferment, and you will need to keep on with it for a week total here. As needed, add in a bit more water and unbleached flour to the mix to feed it some more and keep it going. This will take a week, and even after that is done, unless you plan to use all of the starter at once, you will still need to do once a week feedings to keep the sourdough as good as possible.

You can purchase some of these sourdough starters from the store if you would like, but they are not as good as making some of your own. When you make your own, you get the benefit of going and adding in some of the parts that you want, of knowing what is in the starter exactly and making something that is uniquely yours in each product that you bake. And nothing can beat the satisfaction of that!

Chapter 2:

Getting Your Kitchen Prepared

The next step we need to look at is how to get the kitchen set up and ready to go. If you have already made the sourdough starter that you want to use for the baking, then you are well on your way to making the kitchen ready. There are a few other things that we can organize though to make sure that our bread and baked goods come out perfectly.

The good news is that you probably already have a lot of the basic items that are necessary to bake your first loaf of bread with your sourdough starter. If you don't have one or two of them, you can easily find them online or at your local store. Even those on a budget can go to a local thrift store and find what they need or borrow some of them if you just want to give it a try. A few of the items that you may want to consider to get your kitchen up and ready to go include:

1. Baking pans: Since sourdough is going to use some steam at the beginning to get things going, a certain type of baking pan is helpful.

2. Bread pans that work for loaves are great. You should use an 8.5 by 4.5 inch pan if you are making bread with three cups of flour and a 9 by 5 if you are using four cups of flour.

3. A large rimmed sheet pan. This can be a good way to add to the oven with the bread. Adding ice to it will produce some of the steam that you need here.

4. A baking stone or a baking sheet can be good for breads, like the baguette, that may not fit into the regular loaf pan.

5. A baking dish that is about the size of 9 by 13.

6. A bread lame. This may sound strange, but this is basically a tool that has a handle to hold really sharp razor blades. If you can't find one of these, you can use a sharp knife instead. You would use these to slash through the tops of the bread dough.

7. A 6-quart Dutch oven. This is a good size to use when wanting to bake some round loaves of bread.

8. Food scale: A digital one isn't necessary, but it will make it more likely that you can get success with the sourdough that you are trying to create. Outside of being able to use it to weigh your ingredients as accurately as possible, a scale can be useful when you want to divide the dough or the starter into some good equal parts.

9. Food thermometer: A digital one is best, and this will make it easier to measure out the temperatures of your dough and your water when necessary.

10. Measuring spoons or cups. Dry and liquid ones are good here. They will help you out even when you use a scale.

11. Mixing bowls: The best kind are the stainless steel mixing bowls, just make sure that you don't put the sourdough starter in the bowl before you use it.

12. An oven thermometer: This is necessary when you want to make sure the bread dough will cook well. It is also a good idea to check the calibration of the oven on occasion as well.

These are just a few of the basics that you need to get started with making your own sourdough bread in the kitchen. There are a lot of great options that you can add in, and you can mix and match things based on your own needs. But these simple tools will be plenty to make it easy to start baking your own bread.

Chapter 3:

~

Artisan Loaves

When people think homemade bread, they often think of those delicious, crunchy loaves of bread where the insides are delicate, light, and so decadent, while the outer exterior retains that nice, loud crunch that makes bread so wonderful. No matter the type of artisan loaf that you are interested in, it is absolutely worthwhile to make at least once in your life.

Artisan bread has no classic definition. However, one thing is certain: It is decadently delicious. Typically, it is bread that has a short shelf-life—usually, only a day or two compared to the typical sandwich loaves that people tend to think of. The bread itself is usually stored unpackaged thanks to the hard crust that exists on the outside that can protect the internal soft part. Typically, they have longer fermentation periods in which the bread is able to rise, making them natural choices for sourdough breads.

Within this chapter, we are going to look at all sorts of delicious offerings that you can take advantage of. You will be shown how to make a classic sourdough loaf of whole wheat bread that is highly versatile, delicious on its own, or as bread for a sandwich. You will learn to make many different kinds of breads that you can enjoy in different contexts, looking at rosemary flavored bread, sourdough rye loaves, morning bread, and more. If you like bread that is meant to be eaten fresh and you enjoy the delightful scent of bread baking in your kitchen, check these loaves out for your own enjoyment.

Classic Whole Wheat Bread

What's inside:

- Salt (2.5 tsp.)

- Honey (3 oz.)

- Olive oil

- Butter, melted and then cooled (1 stick)

- Bottled water (.5 c.)

- Milk (1 c.)

- Whole wheat flour (5.5 c.)

- Active sourdough starter (2 c.)

How to make:

1. Take out a big bowl and combine the honey, butter, water, milk, flour, and the active starter. Set this aside for a little bit.

2. After twenty minutes, add in the salt and knead this for a few minutes until it is no longer sticky.

3. Coat a big bowl with some oil and then move the dough to it, turning around to coat. Cover with a towel and then place it into a warm area. Let the dough right for a bit.

4. After three hours, the dough should be double in size. Prepare tow bread pans with some cooking spray.

5. Turn the oven on to 400 degrees. Add some flour to a breadboard and turn the dough out on this. Divide in half and then shape them into the same size as the pans you want to use.

6. Pull the ends, picking up the dough, and slapping it onto the surface as you lengthen it out to be twice the size of the pan. Fold over both halves to the middle and then press down to seal it up. Add into the baking pans and into the oven.

7. After 30 minutes, the bread should be done. Cool the bread for a bit before serving.

Rosemary Bread

What's inside:

- Salt

- Olive oil

- Chopped rosemary (.25 c.)

- Instant dry yeast 92 tsp.)

- Salt (2.5 tsp.)

- Water (1.5 c.)

- Active sourdough starter (1 c.)

- Rye or unbleached flour (5 c.)

How to make:

1. Take out a bowl and stir together the rosemary, yeast, salt, water, active starter, and flour. Knead these together in the bowl for about fifteen minutes to make smooth on the surface but still sticky. Form this into a ball.

2. Coat a big bowl with some olive oil and then move the bread to it, turning to coat it all over. Cover the top of the bowl and then leave it to the side to rise for an hour and a half. It should be double in size at this time.

3. Add a baking stone or a baking sheet into the oven and let the oven heat to 425 degrees. Punch the dough down and divide it into half. Form each of these into a rectangle.

4. Take one of these and fold it halfway to you. Press the edge a bit and fold over one more time, tucking the edges underneath. Repeat with the other piece as well.

5. Spread the loaves with some warm water and sprinkle some salt on top. Flour some parchment paper and add the bread on top. Slowly move these to the baking stone in the oven to bake.

6. After half an hour of baking, you will see the crust is golden brown. Move to a wire rack to cool down before slicing and enjoying.

San Francisco Treat

What's inside:

- Cornmeal for dusting

- Salt (2.25 tsp.)

- Olive oil (1 oz.)

- Bottled water (1 c.)

- Active sourdough starter (1 c.)

- Unbleached bread flour (1 lb.)

How to make:

1. Bring out a bowl with a stand mixer on it, add the olive oil, water, active starter, and flour. Mix these at a low setting for a minute to combine. When this is done, leave the dough in the bowl to set for half an hour.

2. After this time, add the salt and then mix at a low speed for another minute, increase to medium for two minutes and then stop the machine to remove the loose dough from the hook.

3. Cover the bowl with a kitchen towel and then give it time to rise. After two hours, the dough should be double in size. Take it out of the bowl and divide it into two pieces. Form the parts into a bowl until it is nice and tight.

4. Take out two Dutch ovens and line with some parchment paper. Dust the cornmeal on the bottom and then add a ball into each one. Recover the dough and let it rise a little bit longer.

5. After two more hours, turn on the oven and let it heat up to 400 degrees. Use a sharp knife to cut an X into each of the loaves. Then add this into the oven to bake.

6. After 20 minutes, take the lids off the Dutch ovens and then bake a bit longer. After another 10 minutes, take the bread out to cool down before serving.

Italian Sourdough

What's inside:

- Cooking spray

- Beaten egg (1)

- Olive oil for the bowl

- Salt (2 tsp.)

- Unbleached bread flour (4 oz.)

- Semolina flour (6 oz.)

- Warm bottled or filtered water (1 c.)

- Active sourdough starter (1 c.)

How to make:

1. Bring out a bowl with a stand mixer on it. Ad in the salt, bread flour, semolina flour, warm water, and active starter. Let these mix together at a lower speed for 3 minutes or so to get the ingredients combined well.

2. Add some oil to a bowl and coat it all over. Then add the dough and turn it around to get the oil. Cover with a towel and let it rise. This can take up to six hours to finish.

3. Prepare a baking sheet with some cooking spray and sprinkle on the bottom with the semolina. Coat a resealable plastic bag with some spray as well and set aside.

4. Flour a work surface that is clean and turn out the dough on it. Using your hands, stretch the dough out. For it in half and stretch again. Shape into a rectangle, place into a 9 by 5 bread pan, and then place it into the plastic bag. Have it set overnight in the fridge.

5. When ready, take the bread pan out and let it set on the counter for a bit. After an hour, turn on the oven and let it heat up to 400 degrees. Slit the top of the loaf with a bread lame.

6. Put the bread inside the oven to bake. After 35 minutes or so, take it out and let it cool down before slicing and enjoying.

Garlic Bread

What's inside:

- Roasted garlic (1 head)

- Salt (1.5 tsp.)

- Whole wheat flour (.5 c.)

- Unbleached bread flour (4 c.)

- Warm bottled water (1.5 c.)

- Active sourdough starter (.25 c.)

How to make:

1. Take out a bowl and add the whole wheat flour, bread flour, warm water, and active starter. Combine and then cover with a towel to set for half an hour.

2. After this time, add in the salt and knead it with your hands until you get a smooth ball. Spread this out a bit and then add in the garlic cloves, kneading, so the garlic will get distributed without crushing. Cover the dough again and let it set for a bit.

3. After 8 hours of setting, prepare a working surface, and turn the dough to it. Using hands with flour on them, shape the dough into a circle by continually tucking the edges as you make it a ball.

4. Place this into a small bowl that is lined with a kitchen towel with flour. Cover for another hour to rise again.

5. Turn the oven on to 450 degrees. Take out a Dutch oven into the oven. Cust a square of parchment paper and put it over the dough. Flip the dough over and sprinkle some flour on top. Mark an X into the bread.

6. Reduce the heat of the oven down to 425 degrees. Use oven gloves to pull out the rack with your Dutch oven. Remove the lid and put the dough onto the hot pan. Let it bake for a bit.

7. Half an hour later, take the lid off the Dutch oven and then bake for a bit longer. It will only take ten minutes and then remove the bread from the oven. Let it cool before slicing and enjoying.

Greek Olive Bread

What's inside:

- Dried oregano (2 tsp.)

- Parmesan cheese (.33 c.)

- Kalamata olives, quartered (1 c.)

- Salt (1 tsp.)

- Whole wheat flour (.5 c.)

- Unbleached bread flour (3.5 c.)

- Warm water (1.5 c.)

- Active sourdough starter (.25 c.)

How to make:

1. Bring out a big bowl and stir together the active starter and warm water to the starter begins to dissolve. Add the two types of flour and mix well. Let this set for half an hour before mixing in the salt. Let it set again.

2. After two more hours of setting, use your hands to knead the bread inside the bowl a few times. Then let it rest two hours more. Repeat another time.

3. After this is done, add in the oregano, cheese, and olives and knead again to incorporate.

4. Cut out a square of parchment paper and lay it on the counter. Turn the bread onto it and work on the dough to make a ball.

Then move this and the parchment paper to a clean bowl. Cover and let this set overnight.

5. Turn on the oven to 450 degrees the next morning. Remove the dough out of the fridge and sprinkle a bit of flour over this, smoothing it out with your hand. Cut an X into the top of the bread.

6. Move this over, using the parchment paper, to the Dutch oven. Spray with water a few times and place the lid on top. Bake for a bit.

7. After 10 minutes, turn the heat of the oven to 425 degrees and cook for longer. Another 25 minutes, take the lid off the Dutch oven and bake a bit longer.

8. Another ten minutes later, and you can take the Dutch oven with the bread out of the oven. Let the bread have some time to cool down before adding to a wire rack and slicing up.

Morning Bread

What's inside:

- Milk (.4 c.)

- Active sourdough starter (1 c.)

- Warm filtered water (.25 c.)

- Chia seeds (1 Tbsp.)

- Flaxseed (1 Tbsp.)

- Old-fashioned rolled oats (.25 c.)

- Steel-cut oats (.25 c.)

- Rinsed quinoa (.25 c.)

- Room temperature water (.25 c.)

- Melted butter (2 tbsp.)

- Honey (2 Tbsp.)

- Whole wheat flour (2.5 c.)

- Olive oil

- Salt (1.5 tsp.)

- Egg (1)

How to make:

1. Take out a bowl and combine the water, chia seeds, flaxseed, oats, and quinoa. Let these soak for up to eight hours before starting.

2. When this is done, combine that mixture with the whole wheat flour, honey, butter, room temperature water, milk, and active starter. Mix to combine and cover with a towel to rest.

3. After twenty minutes, take out a bowl and coat with oil. Prepare a 9 by 5 pan as well.

4. Add the salt to your bowl and then use your hands to knead it for the next five minutes. Move to the prepared bowl and turn it around to coat all sides. Cover the bowl again and let it set.

5. This takes another three to four hours to rise. When that is done, flour the workspace you want to use and punch the dough down on it. Roll this up, starting on the short end, and then wrap this with some plastic wrap and put it into the fridge to set overnight.

6. The next morning, take this out. In a bowl, beat the egg and brush a bit of it on top of the bread. Sprinkle on the sesame seeds and add to the baking pan.

7. Preheat the oven to 400 degrees. Add the bread inside and let it bake for about 30 minutes until it is done.

8. Allow the bread to cool down for a bit before moving onto a wire rack and slicing up to eat.

Sourdough Rye

What's inside:

- Instant yeast (1 tsp.)

- Rye flour (1.75 c.)

- Bread flour (1.75 c.)

- Molasses (2 Tbsp.)

- Fennel seed (1 Tbsp.)

- Anise seed (1 tsp.)

- Caraway seed (1 tsp.)

- Salt (1.75 tsp)

- Orange zest (1 should be plenty)

How to make:

1. Take your dry ingredients and throw them in a bowl. Add 1.75 cups of warm, not hot, water and mix.

2. Add the molasses and orange zest and mix in the dough mixture.

3. With the dough still in the bowl, cover and let it rest for 15 minutes.

4. Knead the dough once more, and let rest an additional 15 minutes.

5. Knead the dough a final time, then cover and let it rest at room temperature for 14 hours.

6. After the proofing period, take the dough and stretch it out into a round or oval shape to bake. Cover it and let it rest for 15 minutes.

7. Stick the shaped dough into a proofing basket or a bowl with a heavily floured kitchen towel and place the dough inside. Let it rise for about 1.5 hours while covered.

8. Preheat your oven to 475 degrees. While preheating, score the top of the dough.

9. Bake until internal temperature hits 200 degrees.

Chapter 4:

Specialty Breads With Sourdough

There is something special about breads that are meant for specific purposes. From honey loaves that are somewhat sweat amongst the lightly tart taste of sourdough to enjoying rolls with dinner, there are so many different options for you to make. The breads that you will see in this chapter are a bit more niche than the ones that you saw in the last chapter, but that does not make them any more delicious or tempting to consume. These are breads that are meant to be enjoyed and will drive you wild. If you like rolls with your dinners, there are options in here for delicious dinner rolls. If you like apple bread, something sweet that can be great for breakfast or even as French toast, there is a recipe for that as well.

No matter the type of bread that you try here, you will find all sorts of wonderful options for you—you just have to get started. These loaves are simple; you just have to make sure that they are enjoyed by you, nice, warm, and fresh out of the oven. Your family will go wild for these options.

Honey Bread

What's inside:

- Olive oil

- Salt (1 tbsp.)

- Whole wheat flour (1 c.)

- Spelt flour (1.25 c.)

- Unbleached bread flour (2 c.)

- Honey (2 Tbsp.)

- Active sourdough starter (1 c.)

- Warm bottled water (1.5 c.)

- Dry yeast (1.5 tsp.)

How to make:

1. Bring out a bowl with a stand mixer and stir the warm water and the yeast. Add your honey and the active starter and stir it around well. Let this set for a few minutes to proof the yeast.

2. Attach the dough hook to this and then add the salt and the flours inside. Mix on a low setting until combined.

3. Prepare a work surface and turn the dough over to it. Knead the dough to make it no longer stick, adding in some more flour if needed. After a few minutes of that, add the dough into a bowl coated with olive oil and turn it around to coat as well.

4. Cover the bowl with some plastic wrap and then put it into the oven with the light on, but don't turn on the oven. Let this rise for 90 minutes or so.

5. Prepare two 9 by 5 bread pans and set aside. Flour a work surface and add the dough on it. Divide in half and press each into a rectangle before rolling it up on the short sides and adding to your prepared pans.

6. Lightly coat some oil onto two parts of plastic wrap and cover the pans up with this. Put it somewhere warm to rise for a bit.

7. After 45 minutes, turn the oven on to 450 degrees. Take the wrap off the bread and sprinkle with some soil. Cut a diagonal line into the bread and then put it in the oven. Reduce the temperature to 400 degrees while this bakes.

8. After 45 minutes, the bread is done. Take it out of the oven to cool down before serving.

Rye Rolls

What's inside:

- Ice cubes (1 c.)

- Salt (1 tsp.)

- Caraway seeds (1 Tbsp.)

- Rye flour (1.75 .)

- Bread flour (1.75 c.)

- Room temperature filtered water (1.25 c.)

- Active rye sourdough starter (.75 c.)

How to make:

1. Take out a big bowl and combine the water and the starter. Mix well and then add in the caraway seeds with the rye flour and bread flour. Cover this up with a towel and allow to rest for a bit.

2. Twenty minutes later, add in the salt and then knead the bread. Recover and let it set for another 20 minutes. Knead again and add back into the bowl. Cover with some plastic wrap and let it set for another 12 hours at least.

3. Prepare a working surface after this time and turn the dough onto it. Knead for 5 minutes. Divide it out into six parts, being as even as possible. Roll each of these parts into a ball and then cover with a kitchen towel to rise for another 20 minutes.

4. Turn the oven on to 450 degrees. Add a rimmed sheet pan to the bottom rack and place a baking stone on the rack above it.

5. Use a bread lame to slash the top of the rolls and add to the baking stone. Add some ice to your baking sheet and then close the oven to let this melt and turn to steam.

6. Reduce the heat of the oven to 410 degrees and let these cook. After 20 minutes, the rolls are done. Take them out of the oven and give them time to cool before eating.

High-Protein Sourdough

What's inside:

- Salt (2 tsp.)

- Whole wheat flour (1 c.)

- Unbleached bread flour (3 c.)

- Room temperature bottled water (1.5 c.)

- Boiling water (.25 c.)

- Active pumpernickel sourdough starter (.33 c.)

- Chia seeds (1 Tbsp.)

- Flaxseed (1 Tbsp.)

- Quinoa (3 Tbsp. and 2 tsp.)

How to make:

1. Bring out a bowl and combine the chia seeds, flaxseed, and quinoa together. Pour the boiling water on top and let them soak together.

2. In another bowl, combine the rye flour, bread flour, water, and active starter. Cover the bowl with a towel and let this rise for an hour and a half. Then add in the salt before kneading. Cover the bowl back up and let it rest another half an hour.

3. Use your hands to knead the dough four more times. Add the quinoa mixture and knead them all the way in. Add the cover

back to the bowl and let this grow by 50 percent or more. It will take three hours.

4. Cover this up with wrap again and put it in the fridge until the next day. When it is time, turn this onto a clean work surface and shape it into a round boule. Give it time to rest before moving onto some parchment paper. Cover with a towel and let it proof for another hour.

5. Use a bread lame to slash the top of this a bit. Turn on the oven to 450 degrees. Place a Dutch oven inside with the lid on top and let it stay in for half an hour.

6. After this time, pull the rack with this in it out and remove the lid. Move the bread and parchment paper into the oven, and put the top back on. Turn the heat down to 425 degrees and let this bake.

7. After 25 minutes, you can take the lid off the Dutch oven and let it continue to bake for another 15 minutes. When this is done, give it some time to cool down before serving.

Black Pumpernickel Bread

What's inside:

- Ice cubes (2 c.)

- Salt (1.5 tsp.0

- Molasses (3 oz.)

- Lukewarm bottled water (.5 c.)

- Cocoa powder (1 oz.)

- Pumpernickel flour (1 c.)

- Unbleached bread flour (2 c.)

How to make:

1. Bring out a bowl and combine the starter with the molasses, water, cocoa powder, the flours, and the active starter. Cover up the bowl and let it rest.

2. After 20 minutes of resting, knead the salt into the bread for another five minutes. Add a tiny bit of flour if needed.

3. Coat a bowl with some oil before adding the dough into it. Turn it around to coat on all sides. Cover with some plastic wrap and leave in the fridge overnight. Take the dough out of the fridge the next day and let it warm up.

4. Turn the dough to a floured surface. Divide in half and stretch each part out to a foot or so. Work with one piece and fold the short end about three fourths to the other and then fold the

other the same way. Roll one end to the long end and tuck it all in well until it is smooth. Repeat with the other piece. Let it proof for 20 minutes.

5. Turn on the oven to 450 degrees. Add these onto some parchment paper and use a knife and slice it diagonally. Add to a baking sone and into the oven to bake. Add a baking sheet to the bottom with some ice to let it steam.

6. After 20 minutes, rotate the bread around a little bit and close the door. Bake for another half an hour before done.

Apple Bread

What's inside:

- Salt (1.5 tsp.)

- Spelt flour (.5 c.)

- Unbleached bread flour (3.5 c.)

- Room temperature bottled water (1.5 c.)

- Active sourdough starter (.25 c.)

- Ground nutmeg (.5 tsp.)

- Ground cinnamon (.5 tsp.)

- Chopped apples (1)

- Cooking spray

How to make:

1. Turn on the oven to 400 degrees. Add some foil to a baking pan and then coat with the cooking spray.

2. In a bowl, toss together the nutmeg, cinnamon, and apple. Move these to the pan and add to the oven. Turn them over one time during the cooking. After half an hour, take these out of the oven and set to the side, turning the oven off.

3. In a second bowl, stir together the two flours, water, and active starter. Cover with a towel and let it rest for half an hour. After

this time, add the salt and use your hands to knead it together to make a tight smooth ball.

4. Spread the dough out and then distribute the apple pieces a little bit into it, without crushing.

5. Cover the dough with a damp towel and let it rest for another eight hours to double.

6. When this time is up, prepare a clean work surface and turn the dough out to it. Use your hands to form this into a nice round shape and into a ball.

7. Flour a kitchen towel and add it to a bowl. Place the dough into it with the seam up. Cover and let it rise for another hour here.

8. During this time, turn on the oven and heat up to 450 degrees. Place the Dutch oven inside. Cut out a square piece of parchment paper and put it over your dough. Flip the dough over carefully.

9. Sprinkle some more flour on top and use a sharp knife to cut an X into the top. Reduce the temperature of the oven down to 425 degrees. Pull the Dutch oven out and remove the lid. Move the bread on the parchment paper over and cover again to bake.

10. After half an hour, take the lid off the Dutch oven and then let this bake a bit longer. Another ten minutes, and you can take the loaf out of the oven to cool down. Slice the bread up when it is cool and serve.

Toasted Millet Sourdough

What's inside:

- All-purpose flour (3.5 c.)

- Bread flour (3.5 c.)

- Toasted millet porridge (0.75 c. uncooked)

- Sourdough starter (0.5 c.)

- Salt (3 tsp.)

How to make:

1. In a pan or skillet, toast the millet for two minutes. Stir constantly to ensure none of it burns. Occasional popping is expected and okay.

2. Move the millet to a bowl and add two cups of water. Cover and let it soak for at least 5 hours. Millet is ready when you can split the seeds with your fingernails.

3. Take the water and millet into a pan and bring to a boil. Cover and lower the heat to simmer for 20 minutes. Turn off the heat and let the covered millet sit for an additional 10 minutes. Fluff and set aside.

4. Take the flours and mix with 2.75 cups of water. Cover and let rest for 4 hours.

5. Add the sourdough starter to the dough until fully incorporated. Cover and allow it to rest for half an hour.

6. Stretch, fold, and let rest for half an hour. Add salt to a quarter cup of water. Add to the dough along with the toasted millet, making sure it is well mixed throughout.

7. Cover and let rest at room temp for up to 10 hours. When the dough has doubled in size, flour a flat surface and move your dough onto it.

8. Cut the dough in half and shape into your preferred shape. Cover and let rest for 20 minutes.

9. Take a proofing basket and dust with flour. Take the dough and place them inside. If you would like, you can roll millet onto the bottom of your dough before placing it in the proofing basket. Cover and let rest for 2 hours at room temperature.

10. Preheat oven and baking medium to 500 degrees. Transfer the dough into the hot baking medium. Score the top of the dough. Cover and place in oven.

11. Bake for 30 minutes with the dough covered. When time is up, reduce the heat to 450 degrees, remove the lid/cover and bake an additional 10 minutes.

12. Remove the medium from the oven, and take out the bread and place it in a cooling rack. Wait at least an hour before serving.

Sourdough Rolls

What's inside:

- Sugar (1 tsp.)

- Baking yeast (2.25 tsp.)

- Eggs (3, warmed to room temperature)

- Vegetable oil (3 Tbsp.)

- Sourdough starter (1 c.)

- Salt (1 tsp.)

- All-purpose flour (4 c.)

How to make:

1. In a bowl, pour in sugar and half a cup of warm water. Add the year and let sit for 3 minutes. Do not use hot water, as you do not want to kill your yeast.

2. Incorporate two eggs, starter, salt, and oil.

3. Mix in three cups of flour. When everything has combined, add the remainder, a quarter cup at a time. Stop when the bread feels tacky, but not dry. Discard any unnecessary flour when you reach this consistency.

4. Knead until the dough is smooth and springy. Place in a greased bowl, cover, and let it rest until the dough has doubled in size.

5. Take the dough and form a dozen balls. Roll them smooth and place on a greased baking pan. Let the dough rise a second time until the size has doubled.

6. Take your remaining egg and whisk it with a tablespoon of water. Brush this on the tops of the dough rolls.

7. Bake at 375 degrees for 20 minutes.

Chapter 5:

Sandwich Breads

Who doesn't like sandwiches? They are delicious, wonderfully portable options for you for when you want to take your lunch on the go. Maybe you want a sandwich between two slices of bread, loaded up with lunch meat and cheese. Maybe you want a proper sandwich roll to make meatball subs out of, or maybe you are in need of a hamburger bun. No matter the reason behind what you choose out, check these different loaves of bread out—they are delicious, and they can be made in all sorts of different forms.

Just because sourdough bread all has that light, tart taste does not mean that all sourdough loaves are made equal, and this chapter helps to really push that point. You will get to make different loaves of bread for all sorts of different contexts. Do you like Greek gyros? There is an option for pita bread in this chapter. Do you want English muffins to make wonderful breakfast sandwiches? You are in the right place—those are within this chapter as well. If you want a simple loaf of bread to slice up to toss in the frying pan for a grilled cheese sandwich, you have the white and the wheat loaves available to you here. You just have to get started and get enjoying. It is impossible not to go crazy for some of these loaves here—you just have to give them a try. Don't be too surprised when some of these become your new staples, however—when you try some sandwiches on these fresh out of the oven loaves of bread, you will wonder how you ever could have gotten by with the old, preservative-laden store bread that was made in a factory and shipped to you. These breads are worth every single moment that it will take to make them.

Ciabatta Sourdough Rolls

What's inside:

- Sourdough starter (1 c.)

- Instant yeast (2 tsp.)

- Milk (0.75 c., lukewarm)

- Olive oil (1 Tbsp.)

- Salt (1 Tbsp.)

- All-purpose flour (7 c.)

How to make:

1. Using only six cups of flour, mix together all ingredients in a bowl. Add more flour as necessary to get a springy, smooth dough.

2. Cover and let rise until the size is doubled.

3. Poke the dough to let out the gasses and place on a lightly floured surface.

4. Shape into a rectangle and cut into six even rolls. Place on a greased baking sheet, giving them space to expand. Cover and let rest for half an hour.

5. Set oven to 425 degrees.

6. Spritz water on the tops of the loaves and bake for 10 minutes. Reduce the heat to 375 degrees and bake for another 20 minutes.

7. Remove the rolls when they are golden brown in color. Allow them to cool before serving.

Sourdough Sandwich Rolls

What's inside:

- Sourdough starter (1 c.)

- Vegetable oil (1 Tbsp.)

- Egg (1, room temp)

- Salt (0.5 tsp.)

- Bread flour (3 c.)

- Instant yeast (2.25 tsp.)

How to make:

1. Combine all ingredients (using only one cup of flour and leaving out the egg for now) in a bowl and mix well.

2. After a few minutes, add in the egg and slowly begin adding in the remaining flour until dough is firm.

3. Knead for about 5 minutes or until the dough is smooth and springy. Place in a greased bowl, cover, and let rest. If you are able to leave indentations in the dough with your fingers, proceed to the next step. If the indentations disappear, let it rest longer.

4. Place dough on a floured surface and remove the air bubbles. Split into eight pieces and roll them into balls.

5. Place on a greased baking sheet and flatten to roughly a four-inch diameter. Cover and let rest until you can leave indentations with your fingers again.

6. Score the tops of each roll in an "X" pattern. Optionally, make an egg wash (egg and water mixture) and brush the top of each roll.

7. Bake at 400 degrees for about 15 minutes. Remove and let cool.

Sourdough Hamburger Buns

What's inside:

- Sourdough starter (0.75 c.)

- Instant yeast (1 tsp.)

- All-purpose flour (2 c.)

- Rye flour (0.25 c.)

- Potato flour (2 Tbsp.)

- Nonfat dry milk (2 Tbsp.)

- Salt (1.5 tsp.)

- Sugar (1 Tbsp.)

- Unsalted soft butter (4 Tbsp.)

How to make:

1. Mix the starter, yeast, and 0.75 cups of warm water.

2. Add in the flours, salt, sugar, and dry milk. Mix until a sticky ball of dough.

3. Add the soft butter and knead until the dough is elastic and smooth.

4. Cover and let it rest at room temperature for about 4 hours. Stretch and fold to release the gasses from the dough.

5. Lightly flour a surface and divide the dough into six pieces.

6. Roll the pieces into balls and place on a greased baking sheet. Flatten them a tad. Cover and allow them to rise for about 4 hours at room temperature.

7. Set oven to 375 degrees, brush the tops of the rolls with egg wash (egg and water) and bake for about 20 minutes or until golden brown.

8. Pull and set aside and allow them to cool.

Sourdough English Muffins

What's inside:

- Sugar (2 Tbsp.)

- Instant yeast (1 Tbsp.)

- Sourdough starter (1 c.)

- All-Purpose flour (7 c.)

- Nonfat dry milk (0.5 c.)

- Soft butter (4 Tbsp.)

- Salt (1 Tbsp.)

- Citric acid (0.25 tsp.)

- Cornmeal

How to make:

1. Mix together all ingredients save for the cornmeal. Knead until dough is smooth. It should be elastic but not very sticky.

2. In a lightly greased bowl, place the dough and cover. Allow rising for 1.5 hours.

3. De-gas the dough, and place on a floured surface. Allow it to sit a few minutes. Cut it in half and roll them into rounds.

4. Take the cornmeal and sprinkle on a baking sheet. Place the rounds on the sheet(s), dust with cornmeal, and cover. Let them rise for an hour.

5. Take the rounds and place them on an ungreased pan.

6. Cook for about 10 minutes on each side.

7. Remove and cool.

Sourdough White Sandwich Bread

What's inside:

- All-Purpose flour (6.33 c.)

- Sourdough starter (3 Tbsp.)

- Nonfat dry milk (6 Tbsp.)

- Sugar (0.25 c.)

- Salt (2.5 tsp.)

- Instant yeast (2 tsp.)

- Soft unsalted butter (4 Tbsp.)

How to make:

1. Mix a cup and one tablespoon of flour, half a cup and a tablespoon of water, and the sourdough starter into a bowl. Let it rise for 12 hours at room temperature.

2. Mix the remaining ingredients into the above mixture until supple and surface is smooth.

3. Stick in a greased bowl, cover, and allow to rise until doubled in size.

4. Cut in half and roll into ovals. Place them greased bread pans. Cover with greased plastic wrap and allow the loaves to rise about an inch over the edge of the pans.

5. Set oven to 375 degrees and bake for 30 minutes, or until the crust is golden brown. Remove and cool.

Sourdough Whole Wheat Sandwich Bread

What's inside:

- Sourdough starter (1 c.)

- Whole wheat flour (3 c.)

- Salt (1 tsp.)

- Instant yeast (1 tsp.)

- Vegetable oil (2 Tbsp.)

How to make:

1. Mix every ingredient in a bowl until some rough dough is formed.

2. Let the dough rise for 20 minutes, then knead smooth and a bit tacky.

3. Stick the dough in a greased bowl, covered, and allow to rise until doubled in size.

4. Fold the dough a handful of times on a floured surface.

5. Form dough into a log and place in a greased loaf pan.

6. Cover the pan and allow the dough to rise about one inch over the edge of the pan.

7. Set oven to 350 degrees and bake for 40 minutes or until golden brown.

8. Remove the bread and allow it to sit for 5 minutes. Pull the bread out of the pan and allow it to cool completely.

Sourdough Pita Bread

What's inside:

- Sourdough starter (1 c.)

- Bread flour (2.75 c.)

- Olive oil (2 Tbsp.)

- Granulated sugar (1 Tbsp.)

- Salt (1.5 tsp.)

How to make:

1. In a large mixing bowl, throw in the starter, 1.5 cups of flour, and a cup of warm water. Mix until thick. Let sit for an hour.

2. Add the oil, salt, and sugar, and mix. Slowly add in the rest of the flour. Continue mixing until dough keeps to itself and turns into a smooth ball.

3. Place the dough into a greased bowl, making sure to get a bit of oil on the entire exterior of the dough ball, cover, and let sit for half an hour at room temperature.

4. Take one side of the dough and fold it through the middle of the dough ball. Do the same procedure on the other three sides. This will redistribute the yeast.

5. Cover and let sit for 30 minutes, then repeat step 4. Cover and let sit for an hour. Repeat step 4. Cover and allow it to sit for another hour. Check in and see if the dough is elastic and airy. If so, cover and leave in the fridge overnight.

6. Set oven to 450 degrees. Allow a baking sheet to sit in the center rack and preheat with the oven.

7. Take the dough ball and split it into eight parts, rolling them into balls. Flatten with a rolling pin until a quarter of an inch thick and roughly eight inches round. If the dough wants to spring back into itself, allow it to sit for a few minutes and try again.

8. Place the dough balls onto the preheated sheet and bake for roughly three to five minutes. No need to flip the bread, just pull out the pitas and serve.

Chapter 6:

Something Sweet

Who doesn't like sweet breads? While it may seem a bit contradictory to have sweet sourdough bread, these loaves will prove that anything is possible. These are breads that are either designed to be desserts on their own, or they are simply sweet loaves that are delicious on their own or toasted with a smear of butter. As you work through these breads, enjoy every decadent bite that you can.

From making a wonderful chocolate cherry sourdough, filled up with dried cherries and chocolate chips to a loaf of sourdough-based banana bread, there are so many different options for you. Do not be deterred by the fact that you see these referred to as sourdough—they are sweet and delicious. Did you know that you can make sourdough muffins? You will learn how in this chapter! Did you know that sourdough cinnamon rolls are amazingly delicious and surprisingly simple to make? You will learn all about them in this chapter!

Some of the options that you will see in this chapter may even be somewhat surprising—you can make sourdough beignets, for example, light, fried, and deceptively made of sourdough! You can make a crumb cake or a coffee cake—technically not a bread, but still making just as much use out of your sourdough starter as other bread options, so they will be provided as well.

Think of this chapter as a testament to just how wonderfully versatile sourdough can be. The recipes here are diverse, delicious, and so different compared to the other breads that you will be shocked to find that they are actually sourdough in the first place. Give them a shot and see what happens—you will probably discover that you are going to love them just as much as the other loaves.

Chocolate Cherry Sourdough

What's inside:

- Whole-grain rye flour (2 c.)

- Bread flour (2 c.)

- Sourdough starter (0.5 c.)

- Salt (1.5 tsp.)

- Semi-sweet chocolate chips (1.33 c.)

- Dried cherries (1 c.)

How to make:

1. Mix every ingredient in a large bowl. Whisk until well incorporated. Cover and allow to rise for about 6 hours.

2. Move to a floured surface and press the dough into a triangle. Fold it in thirds one way, then the other. It should look like a square, making sure to keep the seam on the bottom. Allow it to rest for half an hour.

3. Take a corner and start folding the sides of the dough under itself.

4. Move the dough over to a floured basket and have the seam face upward. Seal and open part of the seam (you may need to wet your fingers for this).

5. Cover and let sit for up to three hours.

6. Begin preheating your oven at 500 degrees along with the baking medium (baking sheet, bread pan, etc.).

7. Take your dough and flip it upside down onto a cutting board. Score it.

8. Bring out the preheated baking medium and through the dough in. Cover and bake in the oven for 20 minutes.

9. Lower the temperature to 450 degrees and bake for an additional 10 minutes.

10. Remove the lid or top and bake uncovered for another 10 minutes.

11. Bring out and enjoy warm.

Amish Friendship Bread

What's inside:

- Oil of choice (1 c.)

- Eggs (3)

- Milk (1.5 c.)

- Vanilla extract (0.5 tsp.)

- Granulated sugar (1 c.)

- All-purpose flour (4 c.)

- Salt (0.5 tsp.)

- Baking soda (0.5 tsp.)

- Baking powder (1.5 tsp.)

- Ground cinnamon (2 tsp.)

- Instant vanilla pudding (2 small boxes)

- Instant yeast (2.25 tsp.)

How to make:

1. Take a quarter cup of warm water and pour it into a bowl. Add the yeast and let sit for ten minutes. Mix one cup of granulated sugar and one cup of flour. Mix in one cup of milk and then the mixture of yeast.

2. Cover and let sit until it bubbles. Place in a resealable bag and let it sit at room temperature for a day.

3. Place mixture in a larger bowl, add in remaining ingredients (save a half cup of sugar and 1.5 teaspoons of cinnamon), and mix thoroughly.

4. Preheat your oven to 325 degrees.

5. Spray two bread pans with oil.

6. Mix the remaining sugar and cinnamon in a small bowl. Dust the pans with this mixture.

7. Pour the batter into your pans and dust them with the sugar and cinnamon mixture. Place in the oven and bake for an hour or until a toothpick or fork can be pulled cleanly from the center.

8. Cool and serve.

Sourdough Cinnamon Rolls

What's inside:

- Whole or 2% milk (0.66 c. and 2 Tbsp. later on)

- Unsalted butter (4 Tbsp., 2Tbsp. softened)

- Egg (1)

- Sourdough starter (0.5 c.)

- Sugar (0.5 c.)

- Ground cinnamon (3 tsp.)

- Granulated sugar (2 Tbsp.)

- All-purpose flour (2.5 c.)

- Fine sea salt (0.5 tsp.)

- Whipped cream cheese (0.33 c. at room temperature)

- Powdered sugar (0.5 cup)

- Oil or cooking spray

How to make:

1. Warm two-thirds of a cup of milk and two tablespoons of butter in a pan or in the microwave. Mix the egg, starter, and sugar in a bowl while slowly adding in the buttered milk.

2. Now incorporate the salt and flour until a rough dough accumulates—cover and rest for half an hour.

3. Knead the bread until tacky, and it wants to keep its shape.

4. Place the dough in a bowl that has been greased with butter. Cover and let it sit for half an hour.

5. Take a side of the dough and fold it into the middle of the ball. Do this on all sides. Cover it and allow it to rise at room temperature, doubling its size.

6. Lightly oil and flour a surface and move the dough onto it. Stretch and fold the sides into the middle again and turn it over. Pat it a few times and let it sit for 15 minutes. Take a pan and line it with parchment paper. Dust the surface of the dough and a rolling pin with flour.

7. Roll it into a rectangle measuring about 16 by 12 inches. If the dough resists, let it rest for at least ten minutes and then resume.

8. Take 2 tablespoons of butter and melt it. Brush the entire surface of your dough, then sprinkle cinnamon and sugar over the dough.

9. Oil your fingers and roll up your dough down length-wise. Be sure to press down to keep this rolled up and not allow your dough to open back up when baking.

10. Set the roll seam down. Now cut the dough log into sections that are about two inches thick. Allow the rolls to rest an hour or two to let them puff up.

11. Preheat the oven to 350 degrees. Place the rolls on a baking sheet lined with parchment paper and stick the sheet into the center rack—Bake for 40 minutes or until golden brown.

12. Pull out the baking sheet and let the rolls cool for 15 minutes.

13. To make the glaze, mix the soft butter, powdered sugar, and whipped cream cheese in a bowl. Mix until smooth and add milk as necessary.

14. Dust the rolls with powdered sugar and glaze.

Sourdough Banana Bread

What's inside:

- All-purpose flour (2 c.

- Baking soda (0.5 tsp.)

- Salt (0.5 tsp.)

- Soft unsalted butter (1 stick)

- Brown sugar (0.5 c.)

- Granulated sugar (0.5 c.)

- Eggs (2 at room temperature)

- Vanilla extract (1 Tbsp.)

- Bananas (4 ripe and mashed)

- Sourdough starter (1 c.)

How to make:

1. Place the flour, salt, and baking soda in a bowl. Combine and set aside.

2. In a separate bowl, mix your butter and sugars until fully mixed together. Then add the eggs, bananas, and vanilla extract. Mix until the banana mashed thoroughly, with only a few lumps remaining.

3. Add the flour mixture you made earlier along with the sourdough starter. Stir gently.

4. Pour the batter into a greased loaf pan.

5. Set oven to 350 degrees and bake for 55 minutes or until a fork or toothpick can be inserted and pulled clean from the center.

6. Remove from oven and allow to cool before serving.

Sourdough Coffee Cake

What's inside:

- All-purpose flour (1.5 c.)

- Sugar (1 c.)

- Ground cinnamon (an eighth of a tsp.)

- Butter (0.25 c.)

- Sourdough starter (1 c.)

- Oil of choice (0.33 c.)

- Egg (1)

- Salt (0.5 tsp.)

- Baking soda (1 tsp.)

How to make:

1. Combine half a cup of flour, a quarter cup of sugar, the cinnamon, and butter. Mix with your fingers until it all sticks together and is crumbly. Set this aside.

2. Grab your sourdough starter and combine it with the rest of the ingredients in a bowl.

3. Grease a cake pan with butter and sprinkle flour on it, and then pour your batter in.

4. Make sure the top is smooth and then sprinkle the crumbs you made earlier evenly over your batter.

5. Let this sit and rise for half an hour at room temperature.

6. Set your oven to 375 degrees and bake for about half an hour or when a toothpick can be pulled clean from the center.

7. Pull it out and allow your cake to cool before serving.

Sourdough Beignets

What's inside:

- Sourdough starter (1 c.)

- All-purpose flour (3 c.)

- Sugar (0.25 c.)

- Kosher salt (1 tsp.)

- Melted butter (2 Tbsp.)

- Buttermilk (0.75 c.)

- Canola oil

- Powdered sugar

How to make:

1. Combine all the ingredients save for the oil and powdered sugar. Mix thoroughly.

2. Knead until you have made a ball of dough that feels a bit tacky. Lightly grease a bowl, place your dough inside and cover. Let it rise for four hours.

3. Now, take the bowl and let it sit in the fridge for up to 2 days. The longer it ferments, the stronger the flavor.

4. Take a large skillet and start heating with canola oil.

5. Lightly flour a surface and roll the dough out into a rectangle that measures a quarter of an inch thick.

6. Cut the dough into squares and drop the bits of dough into the oil. Do not overcrowd. Flip often to avoid burning. Pay attention not to burn them as they should be golden brown in a few seconds.

7. Allow the beignets to cool and dust with powdered sugar. Serve warm.

Sourdough Blueberry Crumb Cake

What's inside:

Topping

- Sugar (0.25 c.)

- Brown sugar (0.25 c.)

- All-purpose flour (1.5 c.)

- Ground cinnamon (1 tsp.)

- Fine sea salt (pinch)

- Salted butter (1 stick)

Wet ingredients

- Salted butter (1 stick)

- Sugar (1 c.)

- Egg (1)

- Sourdough starter (0.5 c.)

Dry ingredients

- All-purpose flour (2 c.)

- Baking powder (1 tsp.)

- Baking soda (0.5 tsp.)

- Fine sea salt (pinch)

- Sour cream (0.5 c.)

- Fresh blueberries (1 c.)

- Powdered sugar

How to make:

1. Pour the blueberries in a bowl. Add a tablespoon of powdered sugar and combine gently.

2. Take all the ingredients for the topping and put them in a bowl. Mix thoroughly with your hands. Make sure the butter has blended well with the flour.

3. In a small pan, melt butter. A bit of browning is what you want, but do not fully brown the butter.

4. Using a mixer, beat the egg, sourdough starter, and sugar on medium-low. It should take about a minute. Gradually pour in the butter you just melted.

5. In a separate bowl, mix the dry ingredients. Now mix in the wet ingredients on low. Do not over mix this; you still want to see clumps of flour.

6. Add in the sour cream and mix until you have a smooth, thick batter.

7. Lightly grease a pan and line with parchment paper. Begin preheating oven at 350 degrees.

8. Pour the batter into the pan. Sprinkle the crumbles and blueberries evenly. Bake for 55 minutes or until a toothpick comes out clean from the center.

9. Allow the cake to cool and dust with powdered sugar.

Sourdough Blueberry Muffins

What's inside:

- All-purpose flour (1c.)

- Cornmeal (1 c.)

- Salt (0.75 tsp.)

- Baking soda (1 tsp.)

- Ground cinnamon (1.5 tsp.)

- Sourdough starter (1 c.)

- Milk (0.25 c.)

- Egg (1)

- Butter (4 Tbsp. melted)

- Maple syrup (0.5 c.)

- Fresh blueberries (2 c.)

- Coarse sugar

How to make:

1. Mix the dry ingredients in a bowl.

2. In a separate bowl, beat the sourdough starter, egg, milk, maple syrup, and melted butter. Now blend in the dry ingredients and blueberries.

3. Grease the wells of a muffin pan and pour in your batter. Only fill up to two thirds full. Sprinkle sugar over the tops.

4. Bake at 425 degrees for 25 minutes or until you can pull out a toothpick from the center of a muffin clean.

5. Allow pan to cool for 5 minutes, and be sure to pull muffins out to cool separately. Leaving the muffins inside will cause them to keep cooking on the outside, leaving them tough.

Conclusion

And with that, you have arrived at the end of this short guide to making your own sourdough! You might have been surprised at the versatility of a type of bread that was oftentimes just referred to as a sourdough—it truly is diverse, capable of being used in a myriad of ways, and worth every moment of use. While you may find that using the same starter indefinitely seems a bit strange, or if the idea of fermented bread sounds somewhat unorthodox, keep in mind that the loaves that you were provided in this book really are not all that different from the types of loaves that you would make with dry all-purpose yeast. They are delicious and enjoyable. All you have to do is be willing to take advantage of the flavors that they have to offer.

From here, it is time for you to get started. What are you waiting for? Do you have any recipes in mind that you really want to get started with? Maybe you want to start your introduction to sourdough with something light and enjoyable. Maybe you want a dessert option that will fool all of your friends and family into believing that you have made typical breads without the idea of sourdough. There are so many different options for you here—you just have to decide which of the options that you want to take advantage of.

Whether you know that you like sourdough already or if you are interested in trying something new without knowing quite what you are expecting, the introduction of sourdough into your repertoire is a wonderful one to explore. You just have to keep an open mind when you try the options that you have provided to you. Who knows—you may even find that you prefer these methods of bread making to the typical ones. You may find that, once you master using sourdough starters, that you create one that you will pass on to your children and grandchildren as well.

Baking is meant to be shared. We all eat food, and we all love to get close to each other. We love being able to share food together, and we even have expressions such as "breaking bread" with each other when we do sit down to share a meal. It is only fitting that you would make your own new loaves to share with other people as well! Whether you literally break your bread to share it with your friends and family, or you prefer to use a knife to cut it, these loaves will hopefully become recipes that your family and friends talk about for ages. They will hopefully become recipes that are staples in your house that you pass on to your own families. Try to enjoy them, and as you get the experience that you need, try to learn how you can begin to experiment further. Make these recipes your own. Add your own twists or touches to them and begin to enjoy them more than ever.

No matter what you do next or what kinds of loaves that you try to make, thank you for taking the time to peruse through these recipes. Hopefully, you found some that you and your family will really love— every effort was made to create a diverse offering that is not only practical but enjoyable as well. There is something for everyone in this book.

Good luck and happy baking!

Lightning Source UK Ltd.
Milton Keynes UK
UKHW020924010721
386455UK00005B/42